WORDPRESS FOR BEGINNERS

How To Set Up A Self-Hosted WordPress Blog In 30 Minutes

Cyrus Jackson

Table Of Contents

Copyright..................................4

Dedication................................5

Disclaimer................................6

How To Get The Best Out Of This Book..8

Special Gift From The Author...12

Other Books By The Author......15

Second Special Gift..20

Introduction............................23

How To Set Up A WordPress Blog: The Basic Resources You Need..36

How To Install WordPress On Your Domain And Launch Your WordPress Website..................54

An Exclusive Bonus For Reading My Book............................61

Final Thoughts........................66

Do Me A Quick Favour............68

About The Author....................70

Other Books By The Author.......72

Copyright

Copyright ©2017, Cyrus Jackson.

All rights reserved.

No part of this book may be distributed, by any electronic or mechanical means, in print or online, nor may it be altered, plagiarized, sold, loaned or otherwise used for any other commercial purposes without the express written permission of the author and copyright owner.

It's very easy to get permission, just send an email to *Cyrus@onlinebloggingincome.com*.

Sequel to this, monitoring tools has been put in place by the author to check violators.

If you're caught in any way, legal actions you've never experienced before will be taken against you.

DEDICATION

I've always being a big fan of the WordPress content management system and have a big passion for helping as much people as I can master the WordPress platform effectively.

I dedicate this book to every beginners out there who are looking to start a blog on a topic that they are passionate about and build a profitable online business around their blog.

I wrote this book specially for you and hope this book helps you achieve your goals with your blog.

Thank you!

DISCLAIMER

Though, I ensured the information in this book was correct and accurate as at the time of writing, I cannot guarantee with certitude that it will remain so because of how the WordPress Content Management System evolves and the dynamic nature of the internet.

Also, the advice and recommendation in this book are based on my experience and this may change due to circumstances beyond my control.

However, I'll try to update this book when such situation occurs and Amazon will send you a **free** copy to keep you apprised.

But the nature of my busy schedules might cause a little delay because I'm really not **"The Flash"**.

So exercise patience or simply contact me at *Cyrus@onlinebloggingincome.com* or you can post it in the exclusive facebook group: *www.facebook.com/groups/websitetutori*

alcommunity whenever you need a specific clarification.

I'll definitely give you a well-detailed reply.

Also, ensure you check out my other books if you want to learn more about WordPress and setting up a blog the right way because I didn't cover everything you'll need in this book.

How To Get The Best Out Of This Book

Hi there, great to meet you!

I want to personally thank you for buying a copy of this book: ***WordPress For Beginners***.

I really appreciate the trust and believe you placed on me to give you a roadmap to follow to set up your new blog or website on the biggest content management system on the planet: **WordPress!**

This book is a practical guide that can transform you from a total newbie who knew nothing about setting up a website to a professional WordPress builder overnight: from set up, to design; to security and …virtually everything you need to know about setting up a self-hosted WordPress site.

No kidding!

I've laid out this book in simple steps with graphics to guide you where necessary.

So, if you want to get the best out this book, here's what I recommend you do:

- Take your time to read through the whole book, stopping at every step to carry out the specific tasks before you proceed to the next chapter.

  Unless, you actually practice what you've learned in this book, you may not learn what I'm teaching in this book.

- Pick up this book anytime you want to set up a WordPress website for yourself or for a client to guide you along easily. With time, you'll master the whole process quickly.

- Ensure you join my free blogging crash course, ***Blog For Profit Challenge***, which will guide you on how to start a profitable WordPress blog that can earn you $1,000 every single month right from scratch even if you know nothing about blogging which I couldn't cover in this book.

You'll also stand a chance to win a self-hosted WordPress blog to start your blogging career at the end of the course.

All sponsored by yours truly which is my way of saying thank you for participating in the course and motivating you to kick-start your blogging business almost immediately. Here's the link to register:
http://www.onlinebloggingincome.com/free-blogging-course

- I've a special gift **(worth $200)** for you at the end of this book, make sure you don't miss it.

  I love rewarding people that take actions after reading my books.

- Subsequently, use this book as a reference guide whenever you get stuck about any aspect of setting up your WordPress blog.

- Ensure you check out my other books if you want to learn more about WordPress and setting a WordPress website efficiently as I didn't cover everything you'll need in this book.

I'm confident that you will learn a lot of valuable information from this awesome book.

And I assure you: your expectations will not be cut short.

<u>Special Gift For You For Buying This Book</u>

As a special bonus for buying this book, I've a free gift for you: **THE BLOG FOR PROFIT CHALLENGE!**

It's a 15-day crash course on how to start a successful WordPress website or blog right from scratch, even if you're a total beginner without any prior knowledge on how to build a blog the right way.

If you're tired of spinning wheels and creating content that never get read.

Or you've been struggling to dominate your niche and ultimately making money online from your WordPress website or blog.

This is the perfect course for you, so jump right in, to gain free access!

Whether you're just starting out or you're ready to go to the next level with your WordPress website, this course will give you the needed guidance.

WordPress For Beginners

When I launched my WordPress blog: it was a big bang!

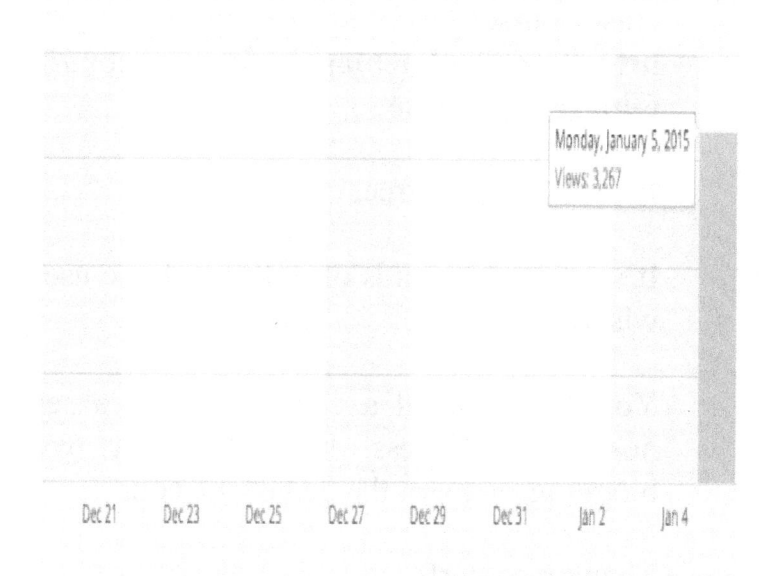

> Monday, January 5, 2015
> Views: 3,267

3,267 unique views on the launch day.

And I would love to share with you the exact strategies that I used to achieve this inside ***The Blog For Profit Challenge!***

Because I'm on a mission to guide you through a roadmap to purposeful blogging and to help you make money consistently from your WordPress blog month after month.

Follow this link to register for the blogging crash course: **http://www.onlinebloggingincome.com/free-blogging-course**

It's all yours for free, enjoy!

It's worth thousands of dollars, please use it wisely.

You'll also stand a chance to win a self-hosted WordPress blog to start your blogging career at the end of the course.

Thank me later!

Other Books By The Author

1. WordPress Security For Webmasters – How To Secure Your Website From Hackers

"WordPress Security For Webmasters" is a step-by-step guide on how to secure your WordPress website (aptly) and keep hackers at bay with an abundance of images, screenshots, and illustrations to give you the needed guidance.

Even if you know nothing about coding or you're not technically-savvy.

With the WordPress platform becoming popular and popular every blessed day, most smart hackers now focus more on the platform and target beginners who have not really mastered the process of securing their websites.

But with this guide, you would go to bed knowing that your website is safe and sound.

I painstakingly wrote this guide in an easy-to-apply manner that frustrates the hell out of hackers and shows you a precise roadmap on how to manage your WordPress website effectively.

Go get your copy right away before it goes up.

WordPress For Beginners

2. *The 5-Day WordPress School – How To Become A WordPress Website Designer In 5 Days Or Less*

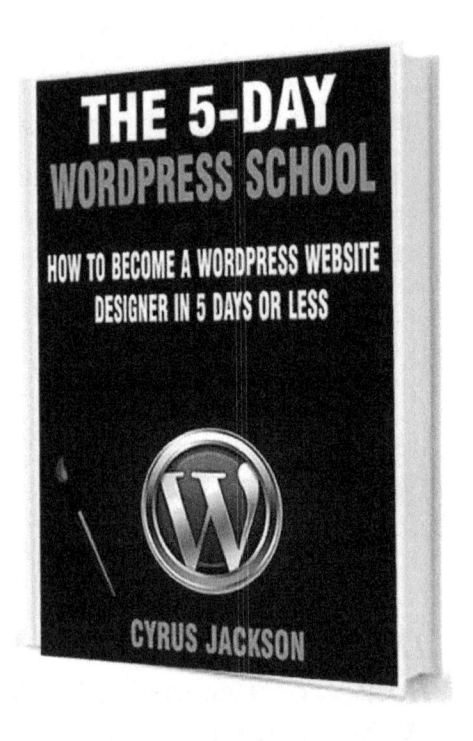

A complete guide on (updated for 2022 and beyond) how to set up professionally, secure aptly and design professionally killer WordPress websites, even if you know nothing about web coding or you're not technically-savvy.

As a professional website designer, I wrote this guide for anyone who wants to build jaw-dropping sites, master every aspect of WordPress and become a professional WordPress website designer.

WordPress For Beginners

With abundance of images, screenshots and illustrations to guide you along where necessary in a step by fashion. Thank you!

Second Special Gift For Buying This Book

Yes, I'm that generous and value you so much as I'm on a mission to ensure you make money online from your WordPress website when you launch it.

I created an exclusive Facebook group for you where you can learn the exact strategies that I use to build my audience on my WordPress website, get support from other smart website owners, and get answers to your questions about any issue regarding your WordPress website.

Also, I share tutorials and guides on how I make money online from my WordPress websites which you can copy and implement for yourself.

Unlike other so-called "experts" who leave you at the mercy of your fate or refer to do some Google search, I'll always be available to answer any questions and ensure you succeed with your sizzling new WordPress website when it's up and running.

WordPress For Beginners

That's my most singular aim for writing this book.

Here's the link to the closed group:

www.facebook.com/groups/Websitetutorialcommunity

With over 5,000 members, you should always get the support you need regarding putting your WordPress website in the right shape, win clients, launch a product, start a profitable online business and build a raving audience that you can turn into customers for your services.

You don't need to pay any website designer or blogging expert a dime as far you are a member of the group **(because you'll become an expert yourself)**, so join right away and your request will be approved within 24 hours!

Here's the link once again:

www.facebook.com/groups/Websitetutorialcommunity

I'll meet inside! Let's go.

WordPress For Beginners

Introduction

5 years ago, I always thought I would need a fortune before having my own self-hosted website?

Yes …believing that only big brands with massive financial "muscles" can have a website.

And the worst part?

Learning coding and all those nerve-racking technical stuff really drove me crazy.

I thought only "web-coding" experts could put a blog online.

But what if there was a way you could build self-hosted blog right from scratch without any prior knowledge of HTML (Hyper Text Mark Up Language) codes or any other nerve-racking technical stuff.

Well, you are in-luck because that's exactly what I'm going to show (in this book) you in a step-by-step fashion with basic screen shots to guide you along where necessary.

Hold on … one second!

Let me tell you a quick story …

5 years ago (from the publication date of this book), I was once like you, a total newbie who knew nothing about website designing neither did I have a website.

I sought for advice and help from every nook and cranny on the internet: Google, Facebook groups, forums etc. without getting a helpful guide.

Most of what I found got me confused rather than enlightened because they were not written in an easy format for a beginner to really understand perfectly.

It was frustrating and energy-sapping.

The worst part was that most so-called "experts" that I contacted were scammers themselves looking for ways to swindle newbies of their hard-earned cash.

Can you imagine?

And yes, I was scammed in the process.

Luckily for me, a mentor (I'll forever be grateful) came to my rescue and offered to help me.

Fast forward to today, I've:

- Helped numerous newbies who new nothing about setting up a Wordpress website with a free step-by-step tutorial without paying a dime to any fat-bellied website designer. It's one of the most popular posts on my website.

    Also, my book: *"The 5-Day WordPress School – How To Become A WordPress Website Designer In 5*

Days" which is a #1 bestseller on Amazon's Content Management System category has helped numerous beginners master the WordPress platform effectively.

- Succeeded in eliminating the fears and excuses of many individuals who want to share their ideas, improve their financial situation and make money from their writing. (This was the main motive I had when launching my website: Onlinebloggingincome.com)

- Earned thousands of dollars monthly from affiliate offers and successfully setting up a website setup business by charging individual who want me to set up a blog or website for their various online businesses.

This has enabled me to sustain myself, pay my bills and live my life while doing something that I love that solves people's problem and end their worries.

Isn't that amazing?

I didn't tell you this to brag or put myself up on a pedestal.

No, far from it.

I shared my story with you to motivate you and give you a sense of believe that: you too can do this!

No matter who you are: **you can set up a WordPress website for yourself and get paid to do so.**

Without going through the nerve-racking journey I went through as you.

I wrote this book so you won't need to go down that road.

So if you intended to start your WordPress website to launch a product, win clients, publish a book or make money online – you're in for a great start.

Get this straight: I'm not talking of a free-hosted blog that comes with ugly, unprofessional and long url like **www.yourwebsite.wordpress.com or www.yourwebsite.blogspot.com**.

I mean a real blog just like *Onlinebloggingincome.com*.

I know starting a blog on free platforms has become the norm especially for beginners.

But the truth is: most of these free platforms come with numerous downsides that will totally frustrate all your efforts.

Just incase, you didn't know. When you host your blog on a free platform:

- Your blog can be deleted at anytime if you violate their ambiguous rules or their system bots mistakenly mark your blog as spam.

    On the 8th of October 2014, Linda Ikeji's blog:

WordPress For Beginners

www.lindaikeji.blogspot.com was deleted by Google because some brands filed complaints on how she violated their copyright images and posts.

But luckily, her blog was later restored when it was found that the allegations were false.

Can you imagine?

The blog was brought down before even confirming the authenticity of the allegations, does that make any sense?

- You can't place adverts on your blog when you start getting traffic or do any form of affiliate marketing which is clearly stipulated in their terms and conditions, unless you're willing to share 50% of your profits with them. That's cruel and inhumane.

They also place adverts on your blog that you can't control, which means they make money from your content while you do all the suffering without earning a dime.

- You can't even use custom email accounts like *Cyrus@Onlinebloggingincome.com* which will demean your credibility and make readers mark you as a spammer.

- You can't use plugins and awesome premium themes to beautify, customize and create a cool template for your website. No wonder all free blogs looks alike.

- You are not really in control because you're on a rented land and have to abide by the strict guidelines and restrictions.

That's why your blog's url usually ends with the host's name like *myblog.wordpress.com* or *myblog.blogspot.com*

In fact, Matt Mullenweg, the founder of WordPress, summed this up in an interview with this conclusion:

"...When you host your site on WordPress.com, it's like renting an apartment, as opposed to a self-hosted WordPress blog that you outrightly own.

With a self-hosted WordPress blog, you can do anything you want. Knock down walls and redecorate it any way you want.

But you're responsible for the upkeep as well (like security updates, feature upgrades...backups etc.). Where as with

WordPress.com everything is done for you but you lose some control. You can't have a yard; neither can you tear down walls ..."

But if you are willing to get it right from the start and invest a few bucks to build an online business from your passion.

You'll definitely leverage the power of an online career to:

1. Become your own boss

With a self-hosted blog, you are in full control and independent because you own your domain.

This means you can monetize your blog according to your preference without going through any form of restriction or strict guidelines.

For example, I'm a website designer and I sell my competence to business owners, schools, bloggers …etc. easily by showing them samples of website that I've built and make cool cash from it.

I dictate the prices and control the services that I render on my blog without any form of restriction, isn't that independence?

2. Customize your blog's design

There are several thousands of themes and plugins available for use on a self-hosted blog for added functionalities and features.

No knowledge of coding is required, as most plugins comes with few-click-installation process to help boost your search engine optimization, improve your blog's speed, embed a forum on your blog, create a membership site and other amazing features that is practically impossible to add on Blogger or WordPress.com.

You just pick up your thinking cap and you can do anything online with a self-hosted blog.

3. Boost your credibility

As you share valuable insights on your blog to your audience, this sends a positive signal to your audience that you know your stuff and positions you as an expert in your niche.

But a free-hosted blog tarnishes your credibility and makes people think you aren't serious.

For example, if you are a new brand or own an e-commerce site, you can win the heart of new customers by leveraging blogging to your advantage above your competitors that just slap up traditional static web pages.

This will build your authority, make customers trust your services and willing to pay for it.

And you know the best part?

You don't need to break the bank to get started with a self-hosted blog or website.

With just few bucks **(about $1 per month)** and some clicks away – you can get started right away.

No overwhelming, complicated or nerve-racking codes to cram.

Just follow the steps below:

"Please note: If you get stuck while setting up your blog with the steps below, feel free to get in touch with me via Cyrus@Onlinebloggingincome.com and I'll be more than willing to help you out."

<u>How To Set Up A WordPress Blog: The Basic Resources You Need</u>

To start your blog or website on WordPress.org, you need the following basic resources:

1. Domain name:

This will be the web address of your blog which people will type in the web browser to access your site. For example the domain name of my blog is ***www.onlinebloggingincome.com***.

When choosing a domain name for your blog, make sure it is:
- Short and sweet. **(3 words is best)**
- Simple.
- Easy to remember.
- Devoid of confusing symbols like ^, - ,~ etc.
- Similar to the focus of your website which tells the visitors what your blog is about.

- A .com extension because most people are familiar with this extension
- Unique and different.

To register a domain name could cost you between $15 and $20 per year but don't worry I'll show you how to get a domain name without paying a dime (for a whole year) when you buy a web hosting account with my recommended web host.

(I'll show you how to go about it below)

2. The WordPress Content Management System

This software enables you to create your blog and write on your blog without any prior knowledge of coding or technical codes.

Just like I said before, it's the best blogging platform on the planet.

3. Web hosting

This is a service that enables your blog accessible online. It helps you acquire a web space for your website.

When choosing a web hosting company, make sure:

- **They have a good amount of disk space**.

Disk space is the amount of content (blog posts, images, videos, slideshows etc.) you can add on your blog. Ipage, the web host that powers my WordPress blog, offers an unlimited amount of disk space so you have no limit as to what you'll add on your blog.

- **They have a good monthly bandwidth**.

Bandwidth is the amount of activities that can be carried out on your blog within a specific period of time (usually monthly): posting comments, reading a post, downloading your book, watching a video on your blog, sharing your post, scrolling a slideshow etc.

When you exceed the specified monthly bandwidth offered by your web host, your blog will be inaccessible until the beginning of another new month and you could lose readers and revenue.

Also, Ipage offers an unlimited amount of monthly bandwidth so you can be rest-assured your blog will always will online.

- **They have a user-friendly control panel**.

The control panel is the area on your web hosting account where you make some necessary settings for your blog like creating a custom email address, installing the WordPress software, adding add-ons etc.

Sometimes, you won't be able to tell if the control panel is friendly until you sign up, so always look for demo to see how it looks.

It's always easier to learn something new when the user interface is easier to understand.

- **They have an effective technical support**.

Preferably a **"live chat support"** where you can get answers to your questions within minutes.

Ipage, a US-based web host, is the service I use to power my blog. Their services are reliable and quite affordable!

They're one the best web host you can find around. They charge **$12 for the first year plus a free domain name registration for life as long as you keep your hosting account with them**.

Also, if you intend to move your WordPress website from another web hosting company to their server; they too this free of charge.

Some hosts charge as high as **$100** for this service.

But in this book, which is catered for beginners, I want everyone to have a WordPress blog without spending too much money on web hosting and domain registration.

So, I would be recommending Ipage because they are reliable, efficient, offer great service and best of all: **affordable!**

Now, you might be wondering: "Why I'm I recommending Ipage?

I recommend Ipage for the following reasons:

- **They offer a 30 days money-back-guarantee**: This shows they're confident of the kind of service they offer so you can just test-drive their service to see things for yourself and if you're not satisfied, you can ask for a full refund: you have nothing to lose.

- **They offer free domain name registration for a whole year**: Ipage offers free domain name registration for a whole year when you buy a web hosting account with them.

  This cuts your expenses and shows that they care about the growth of your business without imposing too many charges on you. That's nice, if you ask me.

- **They offer discounts for new customers**: They offer a discounted price to new customers that buy their web hosting plan which is really amazing.

  Some hosts don't do this, so leverage this one-time opportunity.

  In fact, Ipage is currently running a promo that **offers a whopping 80% discount** for their web hosting plans where you get to pay only $1 per month plus a free domain name registration for life. (I'll show you below!)

  Isn't that awesome?

- **Effective customer support**: They have a live chat support system where you can ask questions whenever you have any issue with your blog. So, you don't need to send emails or support tickets that get responded to after 3 days or more.

You just have to click on the live chat button on their website, start a live chat session with one of their staffs and get answers to your questions within minutes.

I once had an issue with my blog and when I contacted their support using the live chat feature on their website, they were prompt and professional to answer my question and my problem was fixed within few minutes.

They even sent me an email, thanking me for contacting them and asking if everything was okay from my own end.

Amazing, right?

- **Easy means of payment and secured payment platform:** They allow payment with your MasterCard and Paypal and a variety of other means of payments.

So you should have no troubles making payment on their website and their payment platform is very secured.

- **Easy and straight-forward sign up process:** I've actually gone through the sign up process to buy a domain name and web hosting account for my blog on Ipage. And so far, so good ... it's easy to follow and their service has been exceptional. I love Ipage and I'll recommend them to anyone!

- **Free website migration:** While most hosting providers charge up to $100 to move your website from another host to their cloud service, Ipage cherishes its customers so much that they offer this service without any charge, which is incredible.

- **Free $200 in Google advertising credits:** Ipage provides you with $200 in Google advertising credits to utilize to promote your website on Google, Bing, and other search engines.

This will undoubtedly draw a lot of attention to your new blog and significantly increase traffic, which is one of the issues that most new websites experience.

This will significantly increase the earning potential of your site as well as your ranking in Google's search results pages.

Since, I've found the awesome services of Ipage, I've never looked back.

So go to the official website of Ipage and buy a web hosting account right away.

Just follow the following steps below:

(Please Note: I'm using Ipage for this tutorial, but every other hosting provider should have similar abilities. Search their knowledge base or contact their chat support to help you complete the steps using their platform.)

Step 1:

Visit the official website of Ipage which is Ipag.com

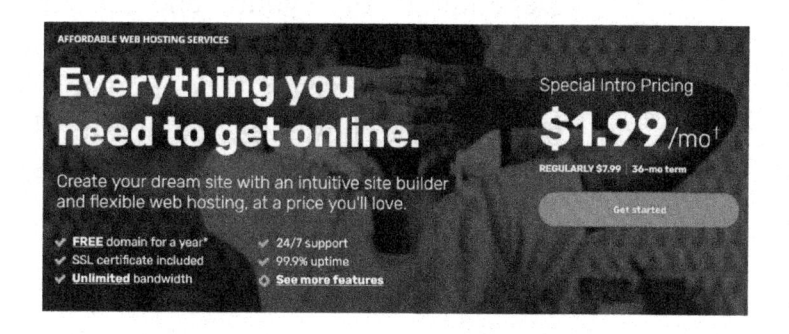

- You'll be taken to a page like the image above. Click on the **"Get Started"** button and you'll be taken to the next page.

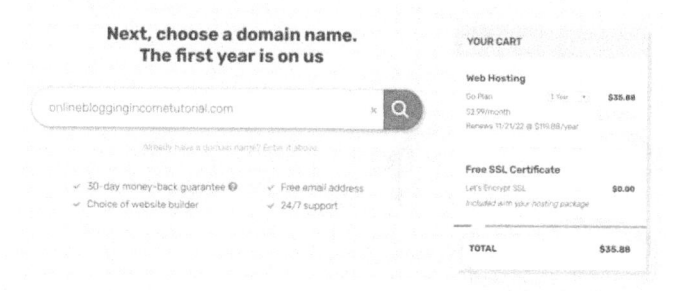

- On the next page, insert the web address of your preference (as shown in the image above, this will be registered for free for a full year) and then select the payment plan of your convenience.

Depending on your choices and spending plan, you can select one, two, or three years. The longer the billing cycle, however, the greater the discount. To begin, select a billing cycle of one year and click "Continue."

- On the following page, Ipage includes some addons such as Website Protection and Privacy. You can remove it by pressing the **X button** because you don't need it.

    You can leave it if you want to add privacy and protection to your domain, but it's not necessary because I'll reveal to you how to secure your site as soon as it gets up and running. Select **"Continue."**

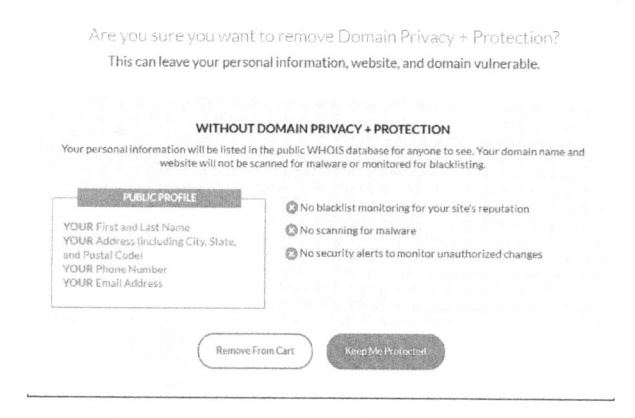

    Are you sure you want to remove Domain Privacy + Protection?
    This can leave your personal information, website, and domain vulnerable.

    WITHOUT DOMAIN PRIVACY + PROTECTION

    Your personal information will be listed in the public WHOIS database for anyone to see. Your domain name and website will not be scanned for malware or monitored for blacklisting.

    PUBLIC PROFILE
    YOUR First and Last Name
    YOUR Address (including City, State, and Postal Code)
    YOUR Phone Number
    YOUR Email Address

    - No blacklist monitoring for your site's reputation
    - No scanning for malware
    - No security alerts to monitor unauthorized changes

    (Remove From Cart)   (Keep Me Protected)

- You'll see a prompt window attempting to persuade you to purchase the addon, but just dismiss it by selecting "Remove From Cart."

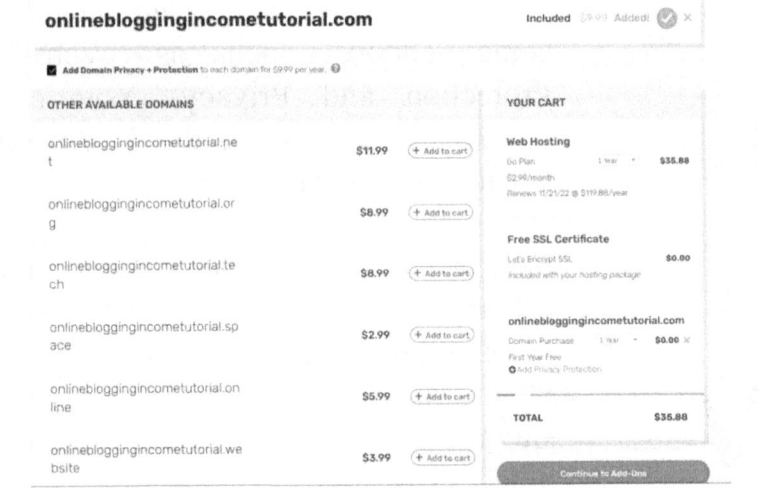

- Then, select **"Continue To Add-ons."**

- Ipage will continue to apply further addons extras (Sitelock and Website Backup & Restore), which you should

WordPress For Beginners

deselect them because you do not really require them.

You can always safeguard your website yourself, and a backup of your site is always accessible in their directory, which you can always access if you have a hosting plan with them.

- You will be sent to the following page as you can see from the image above, where you will enter your payment and account details (First Name, Last Name, Email address, Phone number, Street Address, Country, State).

  Simply include your best email address and phone number since this is where Ipage will deliver your web hosting account information.
  Then input your credit card information or pay using PayPal. When you've finished, hit "Buy Now."

You will get a notification indicating that your purchase was successful.

Please keep in mind that Ipage will send you an email providing your hosting information as well as your login and password. Keep this secure as you'll need it when accessing your control panel.

If you encounter an issue, feel free to send me an email at *Cyrus@onlinebloggingincome.com*

How To Install WordPress On Your Domain And Launch Your WordPress Website

The WordPress content management system must then be setup on your domain name to be fully functional. This will allow you to publish on your WordPress website.

Let's get right into it!

Remember the web hsoting information that Ipage sent to you which I told you to keep safe?

This is the time you would be needing them and anytime you want to make changes to your website from the control panel.

- Visit your domain/cpanel. (Replace "yourdomain with the domain name you registered)

- Enter your **Username** and **Password** to sign in.

You will be transported to your hosting cpanel to install the WordPress content management system.

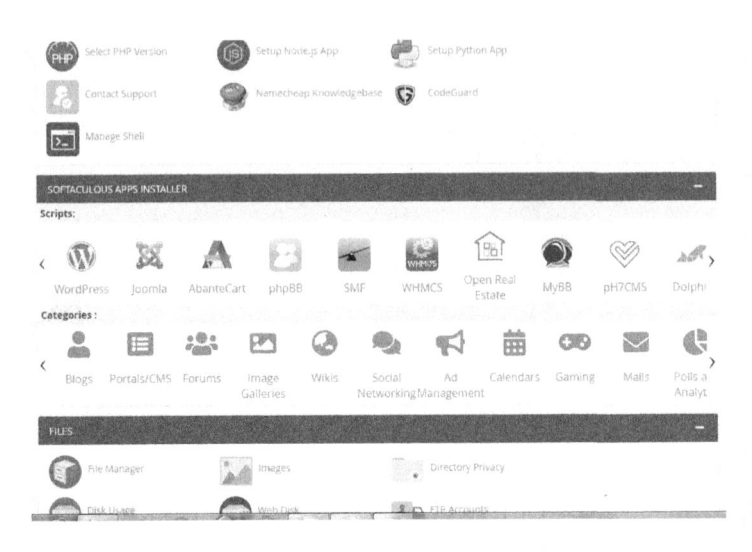

- Scroll down and click on **"WordPress"** under the **"Softaculous Apps Installer"** section.

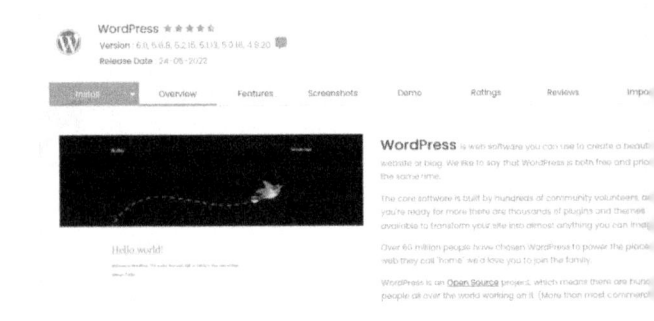

- On the next page, click on **"Install"**.

WordPress For Beginners

You'll be prompted to fill in the details for your WordPress installation and this is how I recommend you fill them so you don't have issues:

- Make sure you select your domain name in Installation URL. Which in my case is **http://onlinebloggingincome.com**

- Enter your **Site Name** and **Site Description**

- Enter your **Admin Username** and **Admin Password**. Make filling in your **Admin Username**, make sure you don't put your domain name there as that's very easily for hackers to guess easily.

Just be creative with it and make sure your password is very strong and easy to remember as well because the details you fill here are what you'll be using to log in to the Admin dashboard of your WordPress website.

- Enter your Admin email. This should be your best email address so you can always get notification regarding your WordPress website.

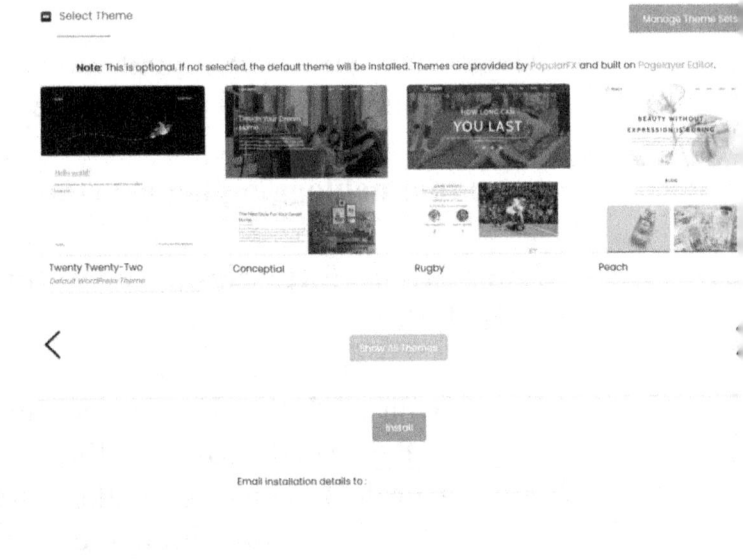

Select your preferred theme and enter the email you want your WordPress installation details to be sent to.

Important Note: Do not choose "admin" or your domain name as your Admin Username because this is what hackers first try out when they want to hack into your website with brute force. Just be creative with it, you get the drift? Also, make sure your Admin Password is very secure.

Finally, click on **"Install"**. When the installation process completes the next page should like this:

Congratulations, the software was installed successfully

WordPress has been successfully installed at :
http://.com
Administrative URL : http://.com/wp-admin/

We hope the installation process was easy.

NOTE: Softaculous is just an automatic software installer and does not provide any support for the individual software packages. Please visit the software vendor's web site for support!

Regards,
Softaculous Auto Installer

If you've finally reached this stage, Congratulations! You've just installed WordPress on your domain name.

You can now start spreading your WordPress blog's link to your friends, family and to the whole world right away!

*If you encounter any problem, feel free to post your questions in the exclusive facebook group: **www.facebook.com/groups/websitetutorialcommunity** or send me an email at **Cyrus@onlinebloggingincome.com** and I'll be more than willing to help you out!*

An Exclusive Bonus For Reading My Book

Remember, I promised you a special gift at the end of this book.

Yes, I don't renege on my promises.

When you sign up with my recommended web host using the tutorial in this book, I'll reward you with a free WordPress website design worth $500.

Most website designers charges anything from **$1000** for this service but it's all yours for free.

Please don't miss out on this great opportunity.

My WordPress blog, *OnlinebloggingIncome*, is hosted with Ipage and I highly recommend their Optimized WordPress hosting based on my experience with them.

With Ipage, you'll get:

- Free custom domain or a free transfer of your current domain.
- Free $200 Google And Bing Ads Credit to promote your website
- Speeds up to 60% faster.
- Unlimited WordPress website.
- Unlimited email addresses
- 24/7 support by phone or live chat
- WordPress experts available to help you whenever you have questions
- Free marketing tools
- And lots more…

Once you provide your proof of purchase **(email confirmation from Ipage)**, I'll provide:

WordPress For Beginners

- Installation of a custom theme.

- Page setup including your Home Page, About Page, Blog Page and Contact Page.

- Website branding including colours and fonts of your choice and your logo if you have one.

- Plugin installation to prevent spam, increase post shares, comment engagement, SEO and list building.

- Custom menus.

- Disclosure and privacy policies pages

- An email consultation (questionnaire) to make sure your website is branded to meet your needs

- Instructions on how to use your new website

To take advantage of this special offer, follow these steps:

1. Open an incognito tab in your web browser
2. Paste the following link in your incognito tab: ***https://bit.ly/Ipagebonus***
   (Using the incognito browser will allow for proper tracking of my link, avoiding any conflict of browser cookies)
3. Scroll down and choose your annual WordPress plan.
4. Choose your new domain or enter the domain you would like transferred.
5. Enter your billing information
6. Choose your extras (you really don't need any of them and can uncheck the SSL certificate, but that's your choice)
7. Submit your order
8. Check your email for the confirmation of payment and forward the email to ***Cyrus@Onlinebloggingincome.com***

Once I verify the order, I'll send you the consultation questionnaire and get started on your website. If you need additional features not listed above, please let me know.

I look forward to working with you and helping to get your new website up and running.

<u>Final Thoughts</u>

You've just joined the league of the smartest website owners.

The whole world is waiting for your words, so don't keep us in suspense for too long.

It was nice holding you by the hand and taking you along the steps you need to give your new website a perfect shape that's different from the norm.

Your company was amazing and I love you to get I touch with me.

Just like everything else you get started with for the first time, you'll need to keep learning as you master the WordPress platform.

If you have any questions regarding what you've just read in this book or any topic related to WordPress and setting up your online platform, I've created a special facebook group where you can post them and meet other people who are just starting out just like you.

Here's the link to the facebook group: **www.facebook.com/groups/websitetutorialcommunity**

And you'll be approved within 24 hours. I'll meet you inside!

Also, do not forget to join *The Blog For Profit Challenge*, my blogging crash course on how to start a successful blog right from scratch even if you're a total beginner or you know nothing about blogging.

Follow this link to gain access right away: http://www.onlinebloggingincome.com/free-blogging-course

Here're ways you can get in touch with me:
(Website: www.OnlineBloggingIncome.com)
(Email:Cyrus@Onlinebloggingincome.com)

<u>Can You Do Me A Quick Favour?</u>

I'm curious and I'll love a feedback from you:

- How did this book deliver on its promises?

- And what kind of doubts did you have before starting to read this book?

Simply let me know by leaving an honest review on Amazon. I love getting feedback from readers in order to serve you better.

Even if it's a few lines, I'll really appreciate it!

Reviews are very important on Amazon as they speak volume of how the book delivered, shows social proof and give others an idea of the content of the book.

So, if you benefited from this book: **drop a review today by following this link.**

WordPress For Beginners

If there's any part of this book you don't really like or you'll like me to add a particular topic you're interested in, please let me know by sending an email to ***Cyrus@Onlinebloggingincome.com*** and I'll be more than willing to help you out.

Thank you, I wish you success in all your endeavours.

About The Author

Cyrus Jackson is an experienced blogger, a passionate author and a professional WordPress builder.

He has been building beautiful WordPress website for the past 5 years and (yes, you guessed it) he's a big fan of the WordPress content management system.

He's also the author of ***Blog Business MasterPlan***, a no-bullshit guide on how to start a profitable WordPress blog right from scratch.

You can join him at ***OnlineBloggingIncome.com***, where he shares his blogging experiences, failures, successes on how you build a profitable online business from a WordPress website.

Other Books By The Author

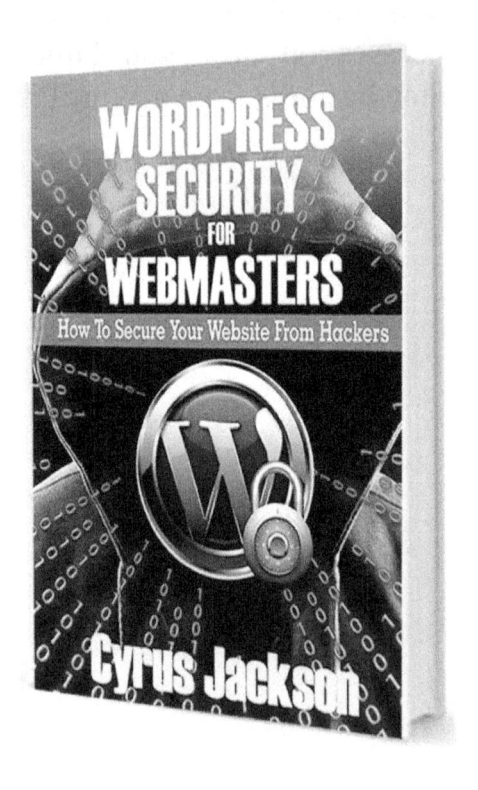

"WordPress Security For Webmasters" is a step-by-step guide on how to secure your WordPress website (aptly) and keep hackers at bay with an abundance of images, screenshots, and illustrations to give you the needed guidance.

WordPress For Beginners

Even if you know nothing about coding or you're not technically-savvy.

With the WordPress platform becoming popular and popular every blessed day, most smart hackers now focus more on the platform and target beginners who have not really mastered the process of securing their websites.

But with this guide, you would go to bed knowing that your website is safe and sound.

I painstakingly wrote this guide in an easy-to-apply manner that frustrates the hell out of hackers and shows you a precise roadmap on how to manage your WordPress website effectively.

Go get your copy right away before it goes up.

THE 5-DAY WORDPRESS SCHOOL

HOW TO BECOME A WORDPRESS WEBSITE DESIGNER IN 5 DAYS OR LESS

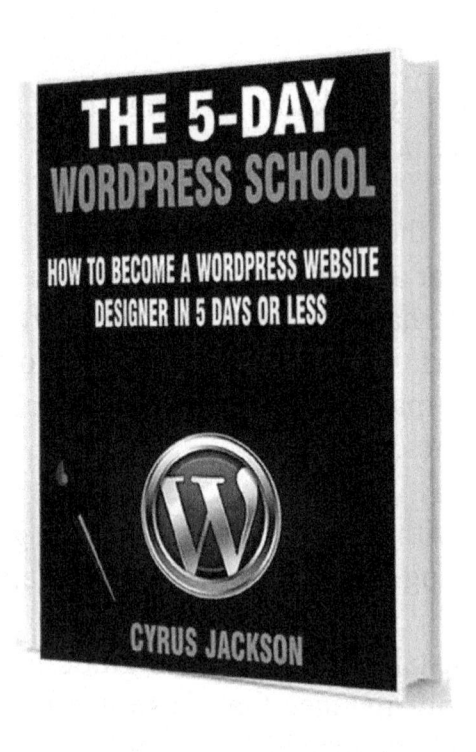

CYRUS JACKSON

A complete guide on (updated for 2022 and beyond) how to set up professionally, secure aptly and design professionally killer WordPress websites, even if you know nothing about web coding or you're not technically-savvy.

As a professional website designer, I wrote this guide for anyone who wants to build jaw-dropping sites, master every aspect of WordPress and become a professional WordPress website designer.

WordPress For Beginners

With abundance of images, screenshots and illustrations to guide you along where necessary in a step by fashion.

Go get your copy on Amazon right away before it goes up!

Thank you!

WordPress For Beginners

Made in the USA
Columbia, SC
27 June 2025